Edinburgh Castle

Chris Tabraham

Principal Inspector of Ancient Monuments

CONTENTS

(1) THE GATEHOUSE

The imposing Gatehouse through which you enter was built in 1888, not to defend the castle but as a conscious attempt to make it look more picturesque. It replaced a plainer, more functional seventeenth-century gate. Within the entrance passage, high up on the walls on either side, you'll see two carved stone panels; these were taken from that earlier gate, and show guns and other military equipment then in the castle, including the giant medieval siege gun, Mons Meg, which you'll see later.

Mons Meg (left) with other guns stored in the castle's arsenal.

Gracing the Gatehouse façade are bronze statues of Sir William Wallace, the victor of the Battle of Stirling Bridge 1297, and King Robert the Bruce, the victor of Bannockburn 1314. They were added in 1929 to mark the 600th anniversary of Bruce's death, though there is no record that either patriot ever visited the castle. The Esplanade beyond was created as a parade ground in 1753.

King Robert the Bruce

(2) THE OLD GUARDHOUSE
&
(3) THE INNER BARRIER

Immediately inside the Gatehouse is the Lower Ward. It is the outermost, and lowest, of the three wards, or courts, that make up the castle. In the Middle Ages, the heart of the castle was in the Upper Ward, high above you on the summit of the castle rock.

The seventeenth-century Inner Barrier was built as a formidable obstacle between the outer and inner gates. It was narrower then, and had a drawbridge and ditch in front of it. The Old Guardhouse began life as a gun platform protecting the Inner Barrier. When the latter became redundant around 1850, the gun platform was roofed over and converted into a guardhouse. When the Gatehouse was completed in 1888, this Old Guardhouse too became redundant. It now serves as the castle gift shop.

The winding road in the Lower Ward leading up from the Gatehouse towards the imposing Portcullis Gate.

This eastern side of the castle, facing Edinburgh's Old Town, was always the most vulnerable to attack and has suffered more siege damage than the rest of the defences. The great wall towering above you, including the awesome curved Half-Moon Battery (16), was built in the aftermath of the Lang Siege of 1571-3. Further improvements to the defences were prompted by the Jacobite Risings of the early eighteenth century.

(4) THE PORTCULLIS GATE

The Portcullis Gate became the principal gateway into the castle following the great rebuilding that followed the Lang Siege of 1571-3. Built over the ruins of the medieval Constable's Tower, the Gate had two outer doors, an iron portcullis and another door at the rear. The stone panel over the gateway is decorated with hearts and stars, the armorial insignia of James Douglas, Earl of Morton and Regent of Scotland, who commissioned the work. The shield displaying the Lion Rampant, the Scottish royal arms, was inserted in 1887, at the same time as the decorative upper storey, known as the Argyle Tower (13), was added.

The sixteenth-century Portcullis Gate marks the boundary between the Lower and Middle Wards.

High up on the wall to the left of the Portcullis Gate is a stone plaque recording the exploits of Sir William Kirkcaldy of Grange, Governor of Edinburgh Castle, during the Lang Siege. To find out more, turn to page 54.

(5) THE LANG STAIRS

This steep flight of steps, aptly named the Lang, or long, Stairs, was originally the main way up into the medieval castle. The 70 steps here now were relaid by prisoners of war held in the castle in the 1780s during the War of American Independence. The curved wall to the right of the stairs may be part of the medieval Constable's Tower, destroyed in the 1571-3 Lang Siege. A plaque high up on that wall commemorates the exploits of Sir Thomas Randolph, Earl of Moray, during the Wars of Independence with England. To read more about that daring escapade, turn to page 51.

The Middle Ward was developed from the fifteenth century on as a service area for the main castle complex crowded onto the summit of the castle rock. Industrial activities such as blacksmithing went on here.

The road itself was formed during the seventeenth century to help the movement of heavy guns in and out of the castle. Further changes to the buildings and defences in the eighteenth century, prompted by the Jacobite Risings, have resulted in this Middle Ward looking much as it does today.

The guns on display (not the original armament) are cast-iron, muzzle-loading 18-pounders, made around 1810 when the wars with Napoleon's France were at their height. You'll see the royal cipher GR3 (for George III) on the top of each barrel.

(6) THE ARGYLE BATTERY & (7) THE CARTSHED

This six-gun battery was the main artillery defence on the north side of the castle. It was built in the 1730s and named in honour of the Duke of Argyll, who led George I's army to victory over the Jacobites at the Battle of Sheriffmuir, near Dunblane, in 1715.

The Battery was built on the orders of Major-General George Wade, best known for his military roads in the Scottish Highlands. The zig-zag fortifications, with embrasures for heavy guns and smaller vertical slits for muskets, were designed by Captain John Romer, a military engineer. The builder, though, was William Adam, the famous architect, better known for designing great country houses but here working as a building contractor for the Board of Ordnance.

The building now housing the castle restaurant was built as a Cartshed after the Battle of Culloden that ended the 1745-6 Jacobite Rising. Originally open-fronted, it held 50 carts that brought provisions to the large garrison from suppliers in the town.

"the third day the gun boomed out at one o'clock exactly, frightening the citizens and scattering the flocks of pigeons roosting on the city's buildings."

(an account of the first successful firing on 7 June 1861)

District Gunner Tom McKay MBE ('Tam the Gun') is the longest-serving (25 years and counting) in a long line of district gunners reaching back to Master Gunner Findlay in 1861.

The time-ball at the top of the Nelson Monument, on Calton Hill, is synchronised with the One O'Clock Gun. At 12.55 hours, the large white ball is hoisted up to the cross-trees, and on the stroke of one o'clock falls back down again. The time-ball actually predates the One O'Clock Gun by nine years (1852).

To the right of the Cartshed (7), on Mills Mount Battery, you'll see the One O'Clock Gun. This signal gun is fired every day (except Sundays, Good Friday and Christmas Day) at 13.00 hours. The citizens of Edinburgh take it for granted and check their watches; visitors jump out of their skins!

The gun was first fired on 7 June 1861 following a frustrating couple of days when the wretched thing misfired. It has continued uninterrupted ever since, except for periods during the two World Wars. The original gun was a 64-pounder muzzle-loader emplaced on the Half-Moon Battery (16). It was linked to the time-ball on Calton Hill (see the panoramic view on page 11) by a 4020-foot (1237 m) long electric cable, weighing 330 lbs (150 kg) and stretching over the city centre at a height of 240 ft (73 m). The combination of the gun firing and the ball dropping served as an audio visual time-signal for shipping in the Port of Leith and the Firth of Forth. The present gun, a 105 mm field gun, installed in 2001, is fired manually; the District Gunner now checks his time from a stop-watch set by British Telecomm's 'speaking clock'!

For the full story, read *What Time Does Edinburgh's One O'Clock Gun Fire?* by Staff Sergeant Tom McKay MBE (alias 'Tam the Gun').

DID YOU KNOW. . .
the only time the One O'Clock Gun has been fired in anger was in April 1916, during World War 1? Its target was a German Zeppelin (airship) dropping incendiary bombs on the city!

DID YOU KNOW. . .
when Mons Meg was fired in 1558, to celebrate Mary Queen of Scots' marriage to the French dauphin, the gunstone was later found on Wardie Muir, almost 2 miles (3.2 km) away?

Ben Lomond

Ochil Hills

Inchcolm Abbey
(12th century)

Scottish American
War Memorial
(1927)

West Lomond
Hill

Forth Rail
Bridge (1890) and
Forth Road Bridge
(1964)

Fettes College
(1840)

Princes Street

Wardie Muir

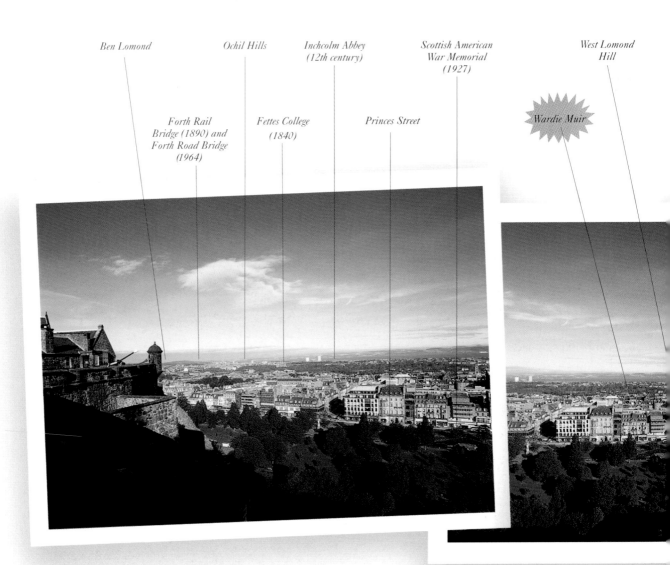

East
Lomond Hill

Royal Scots Greys
Monument (1908)

FIRTH of
FORTH

Port of Leith

Fife Ness

Isle of May

Bass Rock

Kirkcaldy

FIFE

Inchkeith

Lord Melville
Monument,
St Andrew Square
(1823)

Sir Walter Scott
Monument
(1846)

Nelson Monument
(1807)
&
Time-Ball
(1852)

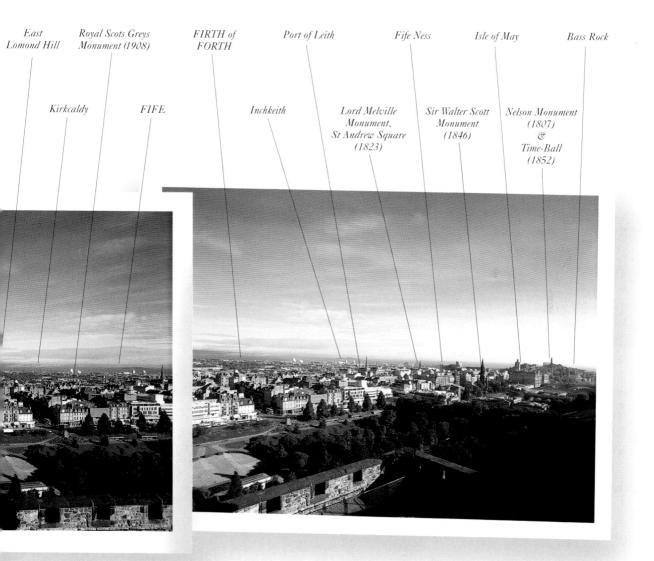

(8) THE GOVERNOR'S HOUSE

This pleasing residence was built in 1742 for the castle governor. Lodgings for the master gunner and storekeeper were provided in the two wings. After the post of governor was abolished in 1860, the nursing sisters of the castle hospital used the building. Today, it serves mainly as

officers' mess with a part reserved for the governor, a Crown appointment restored for purely ceremonial purposes in 1935. (There is no access for visitors.)

It was here on a cold February morning in 1818 that the then governor, Sir George Murray, welcomed Walter Scott and the senior officers of state. Their mission that day was to search for the long-lost Honours of Scotland, the nation's crown jewels (see page 28).

(9) THE NEW BARRACKS

The monumental New Barracks lurking behind the Governor's House provided much needed accommodation for the British army at a time when it was expanding fast to meet the threat posed by Napoleonic France. Work began in 1796, the year Napoleon swept through northern Italy, and was finished in 1799, the year the great general became undisputed leader of his country.

The enormous barracks could house an entire infantry battalion (600 officers and men). It's hardly the finest structure in the castle. Walter Scott likened it to 'a vulgar cotton mill', and his contemporary, Lord Cockburn, was overheard to say: 'Look on the west side of the castle - and shudder!' The seven-storey building still serves a variety of military purposes. (There is no access for visitors.)

A rainwater hopper on the Governor's House bearing the royal cipher of King George III - GR (Georgius Rex) 3.

DID YOU KNOW. . .

the Governor's House was probably where the Ordnance Survey began 250 years ago? General Roy, the Lanarkshire lad who in 1747 embarked on the first methodical military survey of Great Britain, may well have had his office in the master gunner's lodging.

A Victoria Cross, Great Britain's highest award for bravery, on display in the Royal Scots Regimental Museum. Six VCs were awarded to the regiment in World War 1 alone.

I n the vicinity of the Governor's House are three museums devoted to Scotland's proud military tradition.

THE NATIONAL WAR MUSEUM OF SCOTLAND

The **National War Museum of Scotland** was opened in 1933 as the Scottish Naval and Military Museum, the first of its kind in the United Kingdom. This followed the opening of the Scottish National War Memorial (20), and both were in tribute to the men and women who fought in the Great War. One in five Scots who enlisted in the armed services never made it home - a sobering statistic. The museum's outstanding collection presents Scotland's military history from the creation of the first standing army in the seventeenth century down to the present time.

A memento from the Boer War, on display in the Royal Scots Regimental Museum.

Left: A recruiting poster for the Royal Scots (The Royal Regiment), now on display in the National War Museum of Scotland. Edinburgh Castle was the regiment's depot from 1881 to 1964.

THE ROYAL SCOTS REGIMENTAL MUSEUM

The Royal Scots (The Royal Regiment) were officially raised in 1633 when Sir John Hepburn recruited 1200 Scots to serve the King of France - with the blessing of Charles I of course.
In 1661 the Royal Scots returned home to serve Charles II. The original regiment, the 1st of Foot, was known as 'Pontius Pilate's Bodyguard' because of their seniority as the first British Infantry Regiment of the Line.

THE ROYAL SCOTS DRAGOON GUARDS REGIMENTAL MUSEUM

The **Royal Scots Dragoon Guards** (Carabiniers and Greys) were formed in 1971 by the amalgamation of three old and famous cavalry regiments - the Royal Scots Greys, the 3rd Carabiniers and the 3rd Dragoon Guards. The regiment's origins go back to 1678, when the Royal Scots Greys were raised to help Charles II fight the Covenanters (religious dissenters). Their first battle was fought at Rullion Green, in the Pentland Hills on the southern outskirts of Edinburgh.

The Eagle of the 45th French Infantry, captured in the epic charge of the Scots Greys at the battle of Waterloo, 1815. The Eagle is on display in the Royal Scots Dragoon Guards Regimental Museum.

(10) FOOG'S GATE

Foog's Gate dates from the seventeenth century. It was built as the main entry into the Upper Ward, replacing the more difficult route up the Lang Stairs (5).

The origin of the name 'Foog' is unknown. In olden times it was also known as 'Foggy Gate', referring perhaps to the thick sea-mist, or 'haar', that still shrouds the castle rock from time to time.

The wall on either side of Foog's Gate was built in Charles II's reign (1649-85). It has holes for cannon and slits for muskets. Inside, on the left, are two structures built to hold water tanks.

Beyond Foog's Gate is the Upper Ward, the summit of the castle rock. This was the heart of the medieval castle, and of the prehistoric and Dark-Age forts that preceded it. From the highest point, the gun battery beside St Margaret's Chapel where Mons Meg stands 134 m above sea-level, you can get the most marvellous views of the city, the Firth of Forth and the distant Highland mountains - that's if the weather's on your side!

Right: The interior of St Margaret's Chapel looking towards the chancel. The little chapel is still in use 900 years after its construction.

Left: The seventeenth-century Foog's Gate, with the twelfth-century St Margaret's Chapel beyond the oldest building in Edinburgh.

(11) ST MARGARET'S CHAPEL

This little structure is the oldest building in the castle, indeed in Edinburgh. David I (1124-53) built it as a private chapel for the royal family and dedicated it to his mother, Margaret, who died in the castle in 1093. It's just possible that it was originally part of a larger royal lodging. See how the rubble masonry on the entrance side differs quite markedly from the squared ashlar blocks around the other three sides.

The chapel is a delight inside. The fine chevroned arch divides the tiny space into two - an apsidal chancel at the east end housing the altar, and a rectangular nave for the royal family's use. It passed out of use in the sixteenth century and was converted into a gunpowder store; the stone-vaulted ceiling dates from that time. The chapel's original purpose was rediscovered in 1845 and it was restored to its present condition. The stained-glass windows of St Andrew and St Ninian (in the chancel), St Columba, St Margaret and William Wallace were added in 1922. The tiny space is a wonderful place for a christening or a wedding, and the ladies of the Guild of St Margaret maintain the furnishings in memory of their namesake who died here in the castle over 900 years ago.

For the full story, read *St Margaret Queen of Scotland and her Chapel*, by L Menzies *et al*.

"Item, to certain pioneers for their labours in the mounting of Mons furth of her lair to be shot, and for the finding and carrying of her bullet frae Wardie Muir to the Castle"

(from the accounts of the Lord High Treasurer, 3 July 1558)

Beside St Margaret's Chapel stands the giant medieval siege gun, Mons Meg - all six tons (6040 kg) of her.

Mons Meg was one of a pair of guns presented by Duke Philip of Burgundy to his niece's husband, James II, in 1457. The gun was then known

DID YOU KNOW. . .
Mons Meg could only travel 3 miles (5 km) a day, and required 100 men to manhandle her!

simply as 'Mons' for that was where she had been made in 1449. She was at the leading edge of artillery technology, firing gunstones weighing a frightening 330 lbs (150 kg), and designed chiefly to go 'bang' and frighten the living daylights out of the enemy. She was soon in action against the English, at the siege of Roxburgh Castle in 1460, in which James II lost his life. In 1497 she was taken to the siege of Norham Castle, on the English side of the River Tweed. Betweenwhiles, James IV had her trundled over to Dumbarton Castle, on the Clyde, to help teach his own rebellious noble the Earl of Lennox a lesson in loyalty.

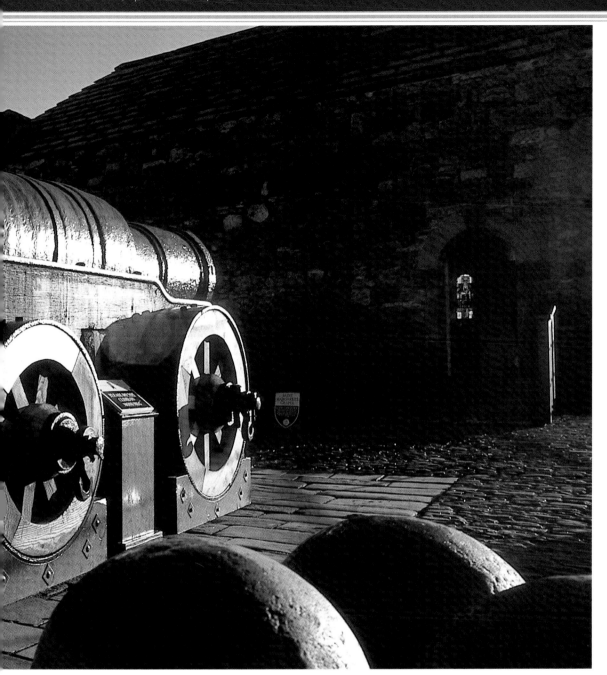

But Mons Meg's great weight made her far too cumbersome, and by 1540 she was taken out of military service and thereafter used solely as a saluting gun. In 1558 she helped celebrate the marriage of Mary Queen of Scots to the French dauphin, François; the gunstone fired that day was later found on Wardie Muir (where the Royal Botanic Garden is today) - almost 2 miles (3.2 km) away!

Mons Meg was last fired on 14 October 1681, in a birthday salute for the Duke of Albany (later James VII). Alas, her barrel burst - you can still see the fractured gunbarrel hoops.

Mons Meg was unceremoniously dumped down in the Middle Ward. And there she lay until she was taken to the Tower of London in 1754, a victim of the Disarming Act that attempted to demilitarize Scotland in the aftermath of the 1745-6 Jacobite Uprising. But her great bulk saved her from being melted down in the furnaces and on 9 March 1829 she was returned to the battlements beside St Margaret's Chapel. Mons Meg, the most remarkable of all medieval guns, had come home.

For the full story, read *Mons Meg: A Royal Cannon* by Peter Lead (1984).

(12) THE DOG CEMETERY

The British are renowned for their love of dogs, and this little cemetery below where Mons Meg stands is proof of that. Since the 1840s it has served as a burial place for regimental mascots and officers' pet dogs.

Here lie such faithfuls as Jess, the band pet of the 42nd Royal Highlanders (the Black Watch), who passed away in 1881, and Dobbler, who for nine years until his death in 1893 followed the Argyll and Sutherland Highlanders around the world to such exotic locations as China, Sri Lanka and South Africa.

Gyp, the Crown Room dog's headstone.

(13) THE ARGYLE TOWER

The Argyle Tower is in effect the upper part of the Portcullis Gate (4). The architect Hippolyte Blanc added it to that ancient structure in 1887. The Edinburgh publisher, William Nelson, who financed the scheme, rather hoped his Argyle Tower might become the permanent home of the Honours of Scotland. He died disappointed.

Left: The Forewall Battery with mighty Arthur's Seat in the background.

Blanc's restoration is an essay in Victorian medievalism. Look out especially for the timber shutter closing an opening in the parapet.

The 'Castles in the Air' exhibition inside features some of the more fanciful Victorian schemes for making the castle appear more romantic; mercifully, most never got off the drawing board!

The tower is named after the ninth Earl of Argyll, who is supposed to have been imprisoned above the Portcullis Gate before his execution on 30 June 1685. Apparently he slept soundly the night before his execution, and went to his death defiant to the end.

(14) THE FOREWALL BATTERY & (15) THE FORE WELL

The Forewall Battery was built in the 1540s on the line of the medieval defences, and substantially reconstructed after the 1571-3 Lang Siege. The Fore Well was the main water supply for the Upper Ward from at least the early fourteenth century. Although 110 ft (34 m) deep, only the bottom 10 ft (3 m) ever held water, giving a capacity of just 2240 gallons (11,135 litres), barely enough to sustain a garrison in siege time. The well was replaced by a piped water supply from the town in the nineteenth century.

DID YOU KNOW. . .
the iron basket on the Forewall Battery wall was used to raise the alarm in an emergency?
In the sixteenth century, one beacon alight meant 'be on your guard'; four meant 'panic - the enemy (ie the English) are invading in strength'!

(16) THE HALF-MOON BATTERY

The curved wall of the Half-Moon Battery gives Edinburgh Castle an appearance unrivalled anywhere else in the world. It was built after the Lang Siege of 1571-3, over and around the smoking ruin of David's Tower, to serve as the castle's chief high-level defence on its most vulnerable east front. Following the 1689 siege, it was repaired much as you see it now.

The Half-Moon Battery is a good place to view the Royal Palace (17). This too was badly damaged during the Lang Siege and lay unused until James VI's 'hamecoming', or return, to the place of his birth in 1617; you can see the dates 1615 and 1616 carved on the building.

Look also at the ornate pediments above the windows. They show royal emblems, including 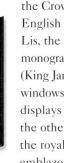 the Crown, the Scottish Thistle, the English Rose, the French Fleur-de-Lis, the Irish Harp, and the monogram IR6 - for Iacobus Rex 6 (King James VI). Between the upper windows you'll see two panels. One displays the Honours of Scotland; the other, now blank, originally had the royal arms of Scotland emblazoned on it.

The Honours of Scotland carved in stone on the Royal Palace.

Left: The Half-Moon Battery and Royal Palace viewed from the Grassmarket

An artist's impression of the Half-Moon Battery being built around the ruins of David's Tower after the Lang Siege of 1571-3 (David Simon).

DAVID'S TOWER

Beneath the Half-Moon Battery lie the ruins of David's Tower. Much of it isn't normally open to visitors because the spaces are cramped and awkward. But part is accessible from the rear of the Battery.

The tower, named after the king who built it, David II (1329-71), Robert the Bruce's son, stood over 100 ft (30 m) high and comprised three storeys of royal accommodation - a ground-floor vaulted strongroom, a first-floor reception hall, and a second-floor bedchamber. Only part of the ground floor remains, for the great tower was brought crashing down during the Lang Siege.

Much of what you see today in the gloomy bowels of the Half-Moon Battery didn't actually form part of David's Tower. The dank cellars were built over the ruin, to serve as stores in peacetime and as temporary barrackrooms during a siege. The thick stone vaults could withstand a direct hit from a mortar bomb. But the cellars couldn't keep out disease, and it was probably here that most of the 70 men killed during the 1689 siege died. The skeletons of 15 able-bodied men discovered in the Lower Ward in 1989 were probably victims of that siege. The casualties also included the lieutenant-governor's cow, wounded by a musket ball!

Crown Square was created in the fifteenth century as the principal courtyard of the castle. The name 'Crown Square' came into use after Sir Walter Scott's discovery of the Scottish Crown and the other royal regalia in the Royal Palace in 1818; before then it was known as Palace Yard.

The castle rock was never a favourite home for the royal family. As long ago as the thirteenth century, Alexander III's queen, Margaret, described Edinburgh Castle as 'a sad and solitary place, without greenery and, because of its nearness to the sea, unwholesome' - no doubt a reference to the thick haar, or sea mist, that still envelopes the rock from time to time. Only when their safety was threatened did they lodge here. A stone plaque in the corner of Crown Square, to the right of the Royal Palace, records the death here on 11 June 1560 of Queen Mary of Guise, during a time of great national tension, the Reformation.

Around the four sides of the square were placed the most important castle buildings - the Royal Palace (17) along the east side, where the sovereign resided; the Great Hall (18) along the south side, the major place of ceremony; the Royal Gunhouse to the west, where Mons Meg and the other great guns were displayed; and St Mary's, the castle church to the north. The last two have long been demolished and replaced - the Royal Gunhouse by the Queen Anne Building (19), and St Mary's by the Scottish National War Memorial (20). Yet Crown Square still retains in large measure its ancient atmosphere of enclosed privilege.

The stone plaque on the Royal Palace in Crown Square, unveiled by Her Majesty The Queen in 1993 on the occasion of the opening of the 'Honours of the Kingdom' exhibition.

Left: The Royal Palace, the residence of Scotland's kings and queens, on the east side of Crown Square.

DID YOU KNOW. . .
such was the grave political situation in 1560 that Mary of Guise's body had to remain in the castle for three months before permission was given for it to be taken to France for burial? Her bones may lie in Reims, but they say her ghost still haunts the Palace!

(17) THE ROYAL PALACE

The Royal Palace began as an extension to David's Tower, but was later enlarged to become the royal residence itself. The last sovereign to sleep here was Charles I in 1633, the night before his Scottish coronation.

Mary Queen of Scots took up residence here in April 1566 pending the birth of her child, the future James VI of Scotland and I of England. Above the round-headed doorway leading from Crown Square to the Birthchamber is a gilded

panel bearing the date 1566 and the entwined initials MAH, for Mary and Henry (Lord Darnley), James's parents.

King James's return to his birthplace in 1617, for his Golden Jubilee celebrations, prompted the complete remodelling of the Royal Palace inside and out. Much of what you see dates from then - the cannon-studded battlemented parapet, and the square turrets with their ogee-shaped roofs. Internally, new state rooms were created, including the Laich ('lower') Hall (recently recreated) on the ground floor, as well as private apartments for the king and queen and lodgings for court officials above. On the first floor, a strongroom, called the Crown Room, was built to house the Honours of Scotland, the Crown Jewels. They are there yet, and have recently been joined by another powerful Scottish icon, the Stone of Destiny, Scotland's ancient Coronation Throne.

Top: Portrait of James VI, attributed to Adrian Vanson, painter at the Scottish court c.1585.

Right: The Laich Hall.

Left: The Birthchamber where James VI was born on 19 June 1566.

27

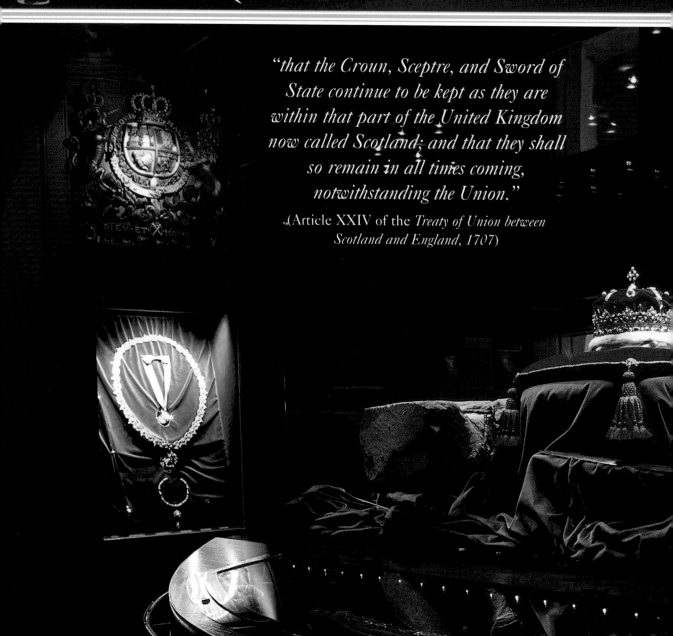

"that the Crown, Sceptre, and Sword of State continue to be kept as they are within that part of the United Kingdom now called Scotland; and that they shall so remain in all times coming, notwithstanding the Union."

(Article XXIV of the *Treaty of Union between Scotland and England, 1707*)

The Honours of Scotland - the Crown, Sceptre and Sword of State - are the oldest royal regalia in the United Kingdom. They were shaped in Scotland and Italy during the reigns of James IV and James V and were first used together for the coronation of Mary Queen of Scots at Stirling Castle in September 1543.

From the time they were taken from Edinburgh Castle late in 1650 for the coronation of Charles II at Scone on 1 January 1651, they have had the most eventful history. For almost ten years they were preserved from the clutches of Oliver Cromwell, first at Dunnottar Castle on the Kincardineshire coast, and then under the floor of nearby Kinneff Church.

After the 1707 Treaty of Union between Scotland and England, the Honours were locked away in the Crown Room. And there they lay for over a century, until in 1818 Walter Scott, with the permission of the Prince Regent (the future George IV), had the room broken into and the oak chest housing them forced open. He found them lying exactly as they had been left 111 years before.

The **CROWN** in its present form was made for James V in 1540 by the Edinburgh goldsmith John Mosman, and first worn by the king at the coronation of his second queen, Mary of Guise, in Holyrood Abbey in 1540.

Left: The Honours of Scotland and the Stone of Destiny on display in the ancient Crown Room. The jewels in the case to the far left are the Stewart and Lorne Jewels, personal regalia of the royal family presented for display in the Crown Room in the nineteenth century.

THE STONE OF DESTINY

*"If destiny deceives not,
the Scots will reign 'tis said
in that same place
where the Stone has been laid."*

(from John of Fordun's *Chronica Gentis Scotorum*)

On St Andrew's Day (30 November) 1996, Edinburgh Castle became the home of another potent Scottish icon - the Stone of Destiny.

The Stone of Destiny had served as the seat on which the Scottish kings had been enthroned, until the English king, Edward I 'Hammer of the Scots', forcibly removed it from its ancient site, Scone Abbey near Perth, in 1296. On its arrival in Westminster Abbey it was enclosed within the Coronation Chair, and for nearly 700 years thereafter was used in the coronation ceremonies of the monarchs of England, and from 1714 the rulers of Great Britain.

Now the ancient Stone of Destiny rests again in Scotland. It will only ever leave when there is a coronation in Westminster Abbey.

For the full story, read *The Stone of Destiny: Symbol of Nationhood* by David Breeze and Graeme Munro, published by Historic Scotland 1997.

The **SCEPTRE** was presented to James IV, probably in 1494, by Pope Alexander VI, and remodelled for James V in 1536 by the Edinburgh silversmith Andrew Leys.

The **SWORD OF STATE** was presented to James IV by Pope Julius II in 1507. The break part-way down the blade was probably made during the smuggling of the Honours out of Dunnottar Castle in 1652.

For the full story, read *The Honours of Scotland: Scotland's Crown Jewels* by Charles J Burnett and Christopher J Tabraham, published by Historic Scotland 2001.

DID YOU KNOW. . .
on Christmas Day 1950 four Scottish students removed the Stone of Destiny from Westminster Abbey? Three months later it turned up 500 miles away - at the front door of Arbroath Abbey, in Angus!

(18) THE GREAT HALL

The Great Hall was built in 1511, with the intention that it serve as the chief place of ceremony in the castle. Sadly it saw little of that. James IV, who ordered it, was killed at Flodden two years later and his heirs much preferred the comfortable surroundings of Holyrood to the draughty heights of the castle rock. When Cromwell captured the castle in 1650, he converted the enormous space into soldiers' barracks, and that's what it remained for the next 200 years. From Crown Square you'll see a blocked-up arched doorway in the centre of the building; that was the barracks entrance.

When the army vacated the building in 1886, work began on restoring it to its former glory. The Edinburgh architect Hippolyte Blanc orchestrated almost everything you see inside - the impressive hooded fireplace, the heavy Gothic timber entrance screen and panelling, the heraldic stained glass, the lighting and flooring.

All that is except the great hammerbeam roof high above your head. That is mostly original and one of the most important medieval roofs in Britain. The stone corbels supporting the main trusses are carved with Renaissance sculpture. Look out especially for the cipher IR4 - for James IV 'Iacobus Rex'; the crowned Royal Arms; Scottish thistles and French fleurs-de-lis, symbolising the Auld Alliance with France; and vases containing both thistles and roses, symbolising the new English connection brought about by James IV's marriage to Margaret Tudor in 1503. (The coats of arms painted on the ends of the secondary rafters purport to be those of the governors of the castle and date from Blanc's restoration.)

"The souls of the righteous are in the hand of God.
There shall no evil happen to them. They are in peace."
(the words around the walls of the Shrine, taken from the *Apocrypha* 3, 1-3)

(19) THE QUEEN ANNE BUILDING

The place where the Queen Anne Building now stands was the site of the Royal Gunhouse in medieval times. It would have been Mons Meg's first home in the castle. By 1700 the Gunhouse had gone, and the present building was constructed following the attempted Jacobite Rising of 1708, during which a French invasion fleet briefly appeared off the Firth of Forth. The building provided accommodation for staff officers as well as barracks for the castle gunners. It now houses the castle's education unit, a café and the entrance to the Prisons of War 1781 exhibition in the Castle Vaults (21).

(20) THE SCOTTISH NATIONAL WAR MEMORIAL

In the Middle Ages, the castle church of St Mary's graced the north side of Crown Square. In 1540 it was converted into a munitions house and eventually demolished in the 1750s to make room for a new barracks. When the garrison left the castle in 1923, the opportunity was taken to adapt the building as the nation's memorial to the dead of the 1914-18 Great War. The architect was Sir Robert Lorimer. The Prince of Wales (the future Edward VIII) formally opened it on 14 July 1927. The building now also commemorates those who fell in World War II and in medal areas since 1945.

The exterior of the Memorial is enriched with sculpture symbolising the 'Just War' - the animals in the windows and niches represent the Vices and Virtues; the humans on the Crown Square elevation signify Courage (mailed figure with sword and shield), Peace (a female with doves), Justice (blindfolded with scales and a sword), and Mercy (a warrior cradling a child). Above the entrance, the figure rising from a phoenix denotes the survival of the Spirit.

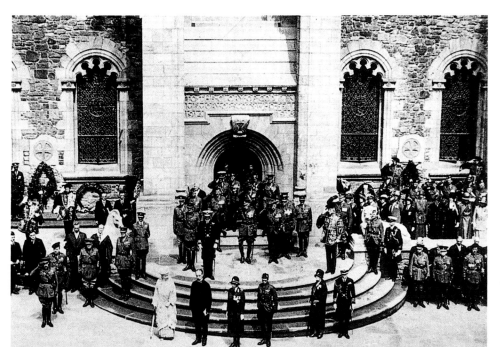

The formal opening of the Scottish National War Memorial, 14 July 1927. Field-Marshal Haig stands framed by the imposing entrance portal. He died six months later.

Far left: above the entrance into the Scottish National War Memorial, the figure representing the survival of the spirit rises up from a phoenix engulfed in flames.

THEIR·NAME·LIVETH

(20) THE SCOTTISH NATIONAL WAR MEMORIAL

Inside the War Memorial is the Hall of Honour, or Hall of the Regiments as it was first called. Here the enormous contribution of Scotland's twelve regiments and the other corps and services are recorded. Beyond lies the Shrine, wherein lies the steel casket containing a complete Roll of Honour of the Scottish dead. The figure of St Michael the Archangel soars overhead, and the stained-glass windows and bronze friezes give vivid impressions of the Great War.

There's one detail so small you could be forgiven for not noticing it. Yet it's perhaps the most chilling in the entire Memorial. High up in a window in the Shrine is the horseman, Faithful and True (from *Revelations*, 19, 15), who 'will defeat the nations, and rule over them with a rod of iron'. On his cloak is a swastika. Hardly had the mortar set in the memorial's walls than the ancient symbol of good fortune began appearing in the skies over Europe, the insignia of a man who too sought to 'defeat the nations and rule over them with a rod of iron' - Adolf Hitler.

For the full story, read *Their Name Liveth: The Book of the Scottish National War Memorial (1985).*

"Yesterday pm about 100 French prisoners were landed at Leith, being part of the crew of the Marquis de la Fayette, *and brought up to the castle."*

(from the *Edinburgh Evening Courant*, Wednesday 27 June, 1781)

The 'Stars and Stripes' carved into a door in the Prisons of War in 1781.

(21) THE CASTLE VAULTS

Crown Square wasn't built on solid rock but on two tiers of cavernous stone cellars. Down the centuries they had a variety of uses - stores for food and military supplies, soldiers' barracks, bakehouses, civil and military prisons.

But it was their use as prisons of war that captures our imagination most. The first POWs, the French crew of a privateer captured in the North Sea by the British frigate HMS *Solebay*, arrived in 1757 shortly after the outbreak of the Seven Years' War with France. By the end of the war they'd been joined by 500 of their countrymen.

The Vaults were pressed into use once more during the War of American Independence (1775-83). Once again, almost all the POWs were sailors, but this time they weren't just Frenchmen, but Spanish, Dutch, Irish - and of course Americans, including two sailors taken from the fleet of Captain John Paul Jones, 'father of the American Navy' and himself a Scot from Galloway. At the height of the war, in 1781, almost 1000 men were imprisoned in the Vaults.

The wars with Revolutionary and Napoleonic France (1793-1815) saw the climax of the Vaults' use as prisons of war. Again most of the POWs were sailors, but soldiers later arrived from Wellington's victories in Spain. They were a mixed lot, and in the crowded conditions feuds developed between the various nationalities. Between feuds, they passed their time playing cards or scratching graffiti on the walls and doors.

For the full story, read *Edinburgh Castle's Prisons of War* by Chris Tabraham, published by Historic Scotland 2004.

(22) DURY'S BATTERY

Dury's Battery, named after Captain Theodore Dury, the military engineer who designed it after the Jacobite Rising of 1708, was used as the POWs' exercise yard. They were left very much to themselves here. Some practiced fencing; others made objects out of old soup bones, bits of wood and bedstraw, which they sold to the Edinburgh townsfolk through the yard's perimeter fence; model ships and intricate little workboxes were the most popular purchases. The more resourceful forged banknotes!

DID YOU KNOW. . .

one prisoner escaped by hiding in a dung barrow, only to be dashed to pieces on the rocks below when he and its contents were tipped over the castle wall? Four more escaped in 1799 by lowering themselves down the rock using their washing lines. But the most audacious breakout occurred in 1811 when 49 prisoners cut their way through the parapet wall; all but one escaped. The hole is there yet.

Left: A ship model (the St George) made by prisoners in 1760 and now on display in the Prisons of War 1781 exhibition. (By permission of the Trustees of the National Museums of Scotland.)

The Western Defences are situated to the west of the Middle Ward.
This area was probably little more than rough grazing ground
throughout the Middle Ages.
It was - and still is - an exposed spot, and was only developed after
1600 to accommodate the fast-expanding garrison.

(23) THE MILITARY PRISON

This prison was built in 1842 to house soldiers from the castle garrison (for offences such as 'drunk on guard'). In the 1880s the building was extended at the rear, increasing the number of cells from twelve to sixteen and providing ablution blocks. A third storey was added for the provost marshal in charge of the prison. The lower cells are now open to visitors.

This little military prison was a miniature version of the great civil prisons of the day. The prisoners were held in solitary confinement and made to do four hours of hard punishment a day; this included working a treadmill, a machine not unlike an exercise bike. After the prison was extended, the regime changed somewhat. The men were still held in 'solitary', but they now did their ablutions outside their cells. And although harsh punishment was still the order of the day, the army doctor now regularly and routinely monitored their physical condition.

(24) THE ORDNANCE STOREHOUSE & (25) THE HOSPITAL

In 1748 a gunpowder magazine capable of holding over 1000 barrels was built on the sloping rock behind the Governor's House (8). It was soon joined by two ordnance storehouses for guns and other military equipment. The powder magazine was demolished in 1897, but the ordnance storehouses were retained and converted for use as the military hospital. Today they are home to the National War Museum of Scotland (see page 15).

(26) THE BACK WELL & (27) BUTTS BATTERY

More soldiers meant more drinking water was needed, and the Back Well was cut out of the rock in 1628. A mere 8ft (2.5 m) deep, it was more a cistern than a well, collecting water draining through fissures in the rock.

Beyond the lower gate in the Back Well Yard is Butts Battery, so-called because it was believed to be where the medieval garrison perfected their archery skills at the 'butts', or target, in the days of William Wallace and Robert the Bruce.

(28) THE WESTERN DEFENCES

Defensive walls have enclosed the precipitous western edge of the castle since at least the seventeenth century. The hazards of patrolling these exposed Western Defences were made clear in a 1677 report which noted that the sentries found them impossible to 'go along in a stormy night'. Even today they can be quite hostile, and for that reason they are generally closed during the winter months.

(29) THE SALLYPORT & (30) THE GUARDHOUSE

It was at the old Sallyport, the back gate midway along the Western Defences, on the night of 19 March 1689 that a secret meeting took place. The Catholic James VII of Scotland and II of England had lately fled into exile and Viscount Dundee, leader of the Jacobite faction in Parliament, met with the pro-Jacobite castle governor, the Duke of Gordon. After the meeting, Dundee rode north to raise an army, whilst the governor began his defence of the castle.

Even though the garrison numbered barely 120 men, and there were just 100 barrels of powder for the 22 guns, they held out against the army of the incoming Protestant sovereigns, William and Mary, for three long months. When Gordon eventually surrendered, just 50 emaciated soldiers remained alive.

During the 1715 Jacobite Rising, the Jacobites almost succeeded in breaching these defences, prompting a fundamental redesign. That's what you see today. The old Sallyport was blocked up, new sentry-boxes built at the angles of the defensive wall (including one intriguingly called the Queen's Post) and a new Guardhouse built for the patrols.

In the 1850s a grandiose scheme was hatched to transform this side of the castle into a 'fairytale chateau'. Work even began. The terrace above the grassy bank of the Western Defences has the date 1858 carved on it, and you can still see the tusking of masonry projecting from it where a fanciful turret was to be built. Mercifully, common sense prevailed and the foolhardy project was killed off before it got any further.

Left: The Western Defences and Queen's Post looking north towards Princes Street. The old Sallyport is immediately below the square plaque.

SYMBOL OF SCOTLAND

*"so strongly grounded, bounded and founded
that by force of man it can never be confounded."*

(from John Taylor's travels around Scotland, 1618)

Three thousand years of history are hidden away in the mighty royal castle of Edinburgh.

In that time the castle rock has been visited by Roman legionaries, Anglian warlords, Saxon princesses, Pictish kings, Norman knights, English invaders and French, Spanish, Dutch, Irish and American prisoners of war.

How and why and when they - and you - came to be here is told in the following pages.

King George IV's triumphal entry into Edinburgh,
August 1822, by John Wilson Ewbank.
(By permission of the City Art Centre,
City of Edinburgh Museums and Art Galleries.)

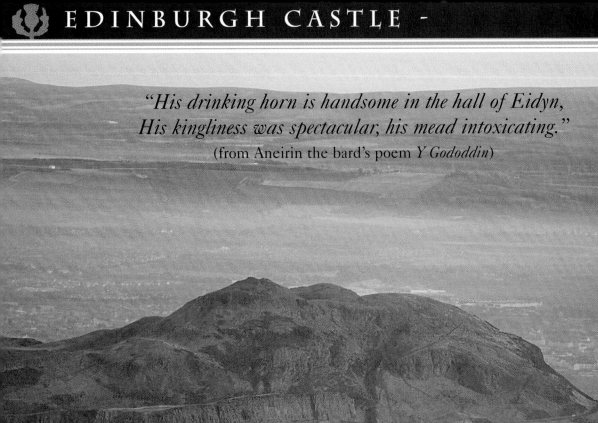

"His drinking horn is handsome in the hall of Eidyn,
His kingliness was spectacular, his mead intoxicating."
(from Aneirin the bard's poem *Y Gododdin*)

The castle rock was created 340 million years ago during a period of violent volcanic activity. Molten magma from deep in the earth's crust erupted into the atmosphere, spreading ash and lava over the land. For several hundreds, perhaps thousands, of years, lava continued to ooze forth, creating a huge cone-shaped volcano. Eventually the volcano died and the lava cooled. Millions of years passed and the volcano became buried beneath layers of sedimentary rock.

2000- year-old bronze brooches found in Edinburgh Castle

Then came the Ice Ages. As each ice sheet passed over the site of the volcano, it gradually peeled away those sedimentary rocks. The last Ice Age, over ten thousand years ago or more, was so powerful that it removed almost everything but the volcano's hard core. The ice, flowing from west to east, gouged out the softer rocks to north and south, the areas we know as Princes Street Gardens and the Grassmarket. But the volcanic rock protected the softer rocks to its east, and by the time the ice sheets merged once more near the site of Holyrood Palace, the world's best-known 'crag-and-tail' - the Castle Rock and Royal Mile - had formed.

Our earliest evidence for humans living on the rock comes in the Bronze Age, about 900 BC. Archaeological excavations conjure up a picture of clusters of large, round houses spread over the hilltop. It seems it was quite a bustling fort by the time Roman legionaries passed by around AD 140, on their way to build the Antonine Wall, Rome's most northerly frontier, west of Edinburgh.

The Romans called the local tribe the Votadini. In time they came to be known as the Gododdin. And it is with them that the castle rock first appears in the historical record around AD 600 - as Din Eidyn, 'the stronghold of Eidyn'. Who or what Eidyn was is a mystery (legend tells of a local giant called the Red Etin), but the rock by then was the stronghold of their king, Mynyddog Mwynfawr 'the magnificent'.

Y Gododdin, a poem by Mynyddog's bard, Aneirin, records a great battle in Yorkshire between the Gododdin and the Angles, recent invaders from Europe and the people who put the 'Eng' into England. It proved a disaster, and only a few made it home, the Angles hot on their heels. Din Eidyn was besieged and taken in 638. The Angles renamed the rock Edinburgh, the English name it has kept ever since.

An artist's impression of life in the prehistoric hillfort around AD 100 (David Simon).

DID YOU KNOW. . .
Mynyddog's warband feasted for a whole year at Din Eidyn before going off to do battle? They drank mead and wine a-plenty from their gold and silver goblets. No wonder they lost!

Left: The Castle Rock and Arthur's Seat, both remnants of ancient volcanoes, dominate the city of Edinburgh. (By permission of Patricia and Angus Macdonald.)

"when Queen Margaret heard the news she commended herself unto God in prayer, and gave back her soul to heaven in the Castle of Maidens on 16 November."

(John of Fordun's account of Margaret's death in Edinburgh Castle in 1093)

Around 843 the Picts and Scots living north of the Forth and Clyde united to become one nation - Scotland. Soon they were making inroads into Anglian territory. In 1018 Malcolm II of Scotland defeated the Angles, or English as they were now called, at Carham on the River Tweed inland from Berwick. Edinburgh was free from English rule at last.

In 1093 we read of a royal castle, called the 'Castle of Maidens', on the rock. Why 'Maidens' is unclear, though there was a story that the Picts used to keep virgins here! In November of that year Queen Margaret was in residence. Her husband, Malcolm III, was away fighting the Normans in Northumberland. Then disaster struck. Malcolm was killed near Alnwick, along with his eldest son. On hearing the tragic news, Margaret took to her bed and died four days later.

In the reign of Malcolm and Margaret's youngest son, David I (1124-53), Edinburgh Castle emerges as a major royal fortress. It was a favourite residence of his, and responsibility for keeping it in readiness for his arrival fell to his constable. Over the centuries the post of constable came to be called governor.

The castle was also the official residence of the king's sheriff, who was responsible for the shire of Edinburgh (the area covered by the present city and Midlothian). From the very beginning there would have been cavernous cellars where the king's rents and dues were stored, and a dark and dingy prison pit for those falling foul of the 'king's peace'.

This early castle was largely confined to the summit, the Upper Ward, and would have been built largely of timber. Only tiny St Margaret's Chapel and the larger St Mary's Church (on the site where the Scottish National War Memorial now stands), where the rest of the castle residents worshipped, were of stone. It seems likely that during the thirteenth century most of the buildings and defences were rebuilt in stone.

But the stone walls were not strong enough to withstand the armed might of the English following Edward I's invasion in early 1296. Their capture of the fortress heralded a new era for the royal castle.

DID YOU KNOW. . .
Edinburgh Castle is the first recorded place where the assembly we now know as the Scottish Parliament met, around 1140?

"Then the English garrison vented their fury overmuch
on the poor common people."
(Abbot Bower describing an action in the winter of 1337-8 after an attempt
by the Scots to recapture Edinburgh Castle)

The castle in English hands was like some festering sore in the heart of the realm. It had to be won back. But how? In the end it took a great feat of daring-do by King Robert the Bruce's nephew, Sir Thomas Randolph.

The assault took place on the evening of 14 March 1314, as luck would have it a dark and stormy night. Whilst the English guards were distracted by a diversion taking place near the main gate, Sir Thomas's assault party made their perilous ascent up the northern precipice.

At their head was William Francis, who as a lad had lived in the castle and knew a secret route over the crags and down into the town that he used to visit his sweetheart. Inching their way up the slippery rock-face, the party clambered over the parapet and into the fortress, catching their enemy completely off-guard.

Following its recapture, the Scots dismantled the castle on Bruce's orders, to make it unusable by the English. Three months later, Bruce won his great victory over the English at Bannockburn.

The great fortress lay ruined and uninhabited for the next 20 years. But on Bruce's death in 1329, war again broke out and by 1335 the castle was back in English hands. And once more it took a feat of bravery and cunning to wrest the castle back. This time Sir William Douglas spearheaded the daring deed.

In April 1341, a ship carrying wine and provisions for the beleaguered English garrison arrived in the port of Leith. On board were 200 Scots masquerading as sailors. The following day, they made their way up to the castle with their consignment.

The garrison, suspecting nothing, opened wide the great wooden gates to let them in. But as the party were passing through, they dropped their casks and sacks to prevent the gates closing and fell upon the startled guards. Douglas and his companions rushed screaming from their hiding - place nearby and helped them overwhelm the rest of the garrison - over 100 men, including 60 archers. They were shown no mercy - their throats were cut and their bodies thrown over the crags.

David II (left) shaking hands with Edward III of England about 1350. (By permission of the British Library - ref: Cotton ms Nero D VI f 61 v)

Shortly afterwards, David II, Robert the Bruce's son, returned to Scotland to begin his personal reign. It fell to him to rebuild the castle his father had ordered to be destroyed, and it is after him that David's Tower is named. King David died in his new castle in February 1371.

Top: A silver coin minted in England during Edward II's reign (1307-27) and found during recent excavations in Edinburgh Castle.

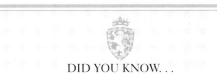

DID YOU KNOW. . .
it took the English three days to capture Edinburgh Castle in 1296? But when they arrived at mighty Stirling Castle shortly after, they found only the castle porter standing there with the keys!

"the castle of Edinburgh, where the King's principal jewels, movables, munitions and registers are kept"

(from an official report dated 1584)

David II's death brought the Bruce dynasty to an abrupt close, and ushered in the age of the royal Stewarts. During their time, Edinburgh Castle became Scotland's most important royal castle.

The emergence of Edinburgh as the nation's capital during the reign of James III (1460-88) was chiefly responsible. James hardly left Edinburgh throughout his adult life, making the castle more or less his permanent home. It was most probably he who replanned the royal residence around a new central courtyard, Crown Square; a rebuilding that reached its stunning climax in 1511 with the completion of the Great Hall by his son, James IV.

By now the ancient castle was not only a royal residence and strong fortress; it was the chief arsenal of the realm, the home of the Honours of Scotland and other royal treasures, and repository of the state archives. It also provided residences for high-ranking officials.

But a castle perched high on a rock, and taking the full force of the North Sea gales, was never going to be the most comfortable of residences. And so the Stewarts cast their eyes on the abbey of Holyrood down at the far end of the Royal Mile and decided that was more to their liking. Their predecessors had long made the abbey's guest range their own unofficial Edinburgh residence; now as the Reformation approached, and the number of Augustinian canons dwindled, they made it official. The draughty castle would henceforth only be used as a royal residence when security or protocol demanded.

The castle from the Vennel, Grassmarket.

Both factors combined in 1566 when it was proclaimed that Mary Queen of Scots was expecting a child, an heir to the throne not only of Scotland but of England and Ireland also. Mary took up residence in the castle in April, and here, in the cramped seclusion of the Birthchamber, on the morning of Wednesday 19 June she gave birth to Prince James. The infant, who in 1603 would unite the Crowns of Scotland and England, was taken from the chamber and presented to the representatives of a thankful nation.

Mary Queen of Scots (1542-87), by an unknown artist.

DID YOU KNOW. . .

Elizabeth of England, the 'Virgin Queen' and Mary's cousin, on hearing the news of Prince James's birth in 1566, sighed and said: 'The queen of Scots is lighter of a bonny son, and I am but barren stock.' ? Thirty-seven years later, the 'bonny son' succeeded her as sovereign of England.

"no mining can prevail in this rock but only battery with ordnance to beat down the walls."
(an English spy's assessment of the castle's formidable strength in April 1573)

On 6 May 1567, Mary Queen of Scots entered the castle with the Earl of Bothwell. The guns 'schot maist magnificentlie' to welcome them. Nine days later they were married. The union, though, was a disaster and provoked Mary's nobles to rebel. She was soon caught and imprisoned in Lochleven Castle, near Kinross, where she was forced to abdicate in favour of her son, James VI. Escaping her watery prison ten months later, she fought and lost her last battle at Langside, near Glasgow, before fleeing to England and the safety, so she thought, of her cousin, Queen Elizabeth.

Despite her departure, there were still those in Scotland who continued to support her cause - among them Sir William Kirkcaldy of Grange, governor of Edinburgh Castle. By the summer of 1571 he was defiantly holding the fortress against the regent governing on behalf of the infant James. The siege dragged on for well over a year - hence its name, the Lang (or long) Siege - until in 1573 the besiegers sought help from Queen Elizabeth.

Twenty heavy guns were duly despatched from Berwick, and a ring of six batteries was drawn like a noose around the castle. Within ten days of the massive bombardment commencing on 16 May, much of the east side of the castle was brought crashing down, including David's Tower and Constable's Tower. With the Fore Well choked with rubble, Kirkcaldy had no option but to surrender.

Most of the beleaguered garrison were allowed to go free. Not poor Sir William. The great soldier, of whom a fellow Scot remarked that he was 'like a lamb in the house but like a lion in the field', was ignominiously hauled behind a cart through the streets of Edinburgh to the mercat cross in the Royal Mile and executed. His severed head was impaled on a spike on the ruined castle walls he'd so resolutely defended for his queen.

DID YOU KNOW. . .
one cannonball fired from the battlements in 1573 blew the baskets in the Fish Market, near St Giles' Church, so high into the air that their contents landed on the rooftops of the ten-storey-high houses nearby?

'There are armed men and cannon in the citadel overhead;
you may see the troops marshalled on the high parade;
and at night after the early winter evenfall,
and in the morning before the laggard winter dawn,
the wind carries abroad over Edinburgh
the sound of drums and bugles.'
(from Robert Louis Stevenson, *Edinburgh, Picturesque Notes*, 1878)

In 1633, James VI's son, Charles I, slept in the castle the night before his Scottish coronation. It was the last occasion a reigning sovereign stayed here. Charles's execution in 1649, and the unequivocal support of the Scots for his rightful successor, Charles II, brought Oliver Cromwell to Scotland. By Christmas Day 1650 the Lord Protector of England had set up his headquarters here in the castle.

The ancient castle now began to take on the appearance of a garrison fortress. Before Cromwell's time, the Scottish 'host', or army, had been called out only when the need arose, and the castle was 'stuffed with men' only in times of crisis. But from now on it would have a permanent garrison of soldiers stationed here.

Much of what you see today dates from the seventeenth century and later. Some important medieval buildings were demolished, including the Royal Gunhouse in 1708 (to make way for the Queen Anne Building) and St Mary's Church in 1755 (on the site of the Scottish National War Memorial), others were converted, and new ones erected. Almost every inch of space was given over to army use, including James VI's Birthchamber - as a small-arms store.

The defences too were radically rebuilt, for the castle was still a key military target. The five Jacobite Risings that followed in the wake of James VII's flight into exile in 1689 (the word Jacobite comes from 'Iacobus', Latin for James) made that all too clear.

Left: Edinburgh Castle around 1745, by an unknown artist.

Below: The soldiers' mess in the Castle, 1882 by RG Hutchison. (By permission of the Trustees of the National Museums of Scotland)

DID YOU KNOW. . .
that the only room in the castle not requisitioned by the garrison was the Crown Room? Probably because the door had been locked after the Act of Union in 1707 and nobody could find the keys!

'*He who pretends to my throne*'.
(Queen Anne (1702-14) referring to her
half-brother, and rival for the British throne,
James Francis Edward Stewart,
the 'Old Pretender')

The Jacobites weren't long in losing control of their departed sovereign's castle. Despite a determined resistance in the early months of 1689, during which over 70 men lost their lives, by June the Jacobite governor, the Duke of Gordon, was compelled to surrender to the forces loyal to the incoming sovereigns, William and Mary. An attempted Jacobite Rising in 1708 failed before it had even begun, but in 1715, hot on the heels of the accession of George I, the Elector of Hanover, to the British throne, the Jacobites almost succeeded in retaking Edinburgh Castle.

The Jacobite plan was to scale the precipitous rock face on the Western Defences and break in through the Sallyport, where the Duke of Gordon and Viscount Dundee had held their clandestine meeting in 1689. All initially went well. A sergeant and two privates serving in the castle were bribed into colluding with them and the Jacobites, under Lord Drummond, prepared to make their attempt.

Above: A contemporary depiction of the Jacobite attempt to capture the castle in 1715.

Under the cover of darkness, Drummond's men picked their way up the sheer rock face and arrived at the base of the castle walls - though how the one-legged Captain Maclean, a veteran of Killiecrankie, made it up beggars belief! With them they had a ladder sufficient, so they thought, to reach over the high wall. Unfortunately, Captain Forbes had failed to arrive with his section of ladder, but Drummond decided to make the attempt anyway. What followed was sheer farce, for the ladder was too short! To add to their woes, the officer of the watch decided to make his rounds earlier than usual and saw the two colluding privates wrestling with the stunted ladder. Realising they'd been spotted, the two tried to save their own necks by throwing down the ropes. The ladder and all on it fell heavily onto the rock below. So near - and yet so far - had Scotland's chief garrison fortress come from being taken.

The attempt, although a failure, gave the military authorities a fright. As a result, the artillery defences around the north and west sides were rebuilt much as you see them today. They were put to the test during the 1745 Rising, but only in a desultory way, for Bonnie Prince Charlie didn't have any heavy guns to make a serious attempt. His effort proved to be the last military action the castle saw. Thereafter, the castle garrison was chiefly concerned with preparing to go overseas to fight for the fast-expanding British Empire.

Left: James Francis Edward Stewart, the 'Old Pretender', contemplating an expedition to regain his lost British throne; a painting attributed to Francesco Trevisani.

On his breastplate, James wears the St Andrew Jewel of the Order of the Thistle. Following the death of his younger son, Prince Henry, in 1807, that jewel (see inset) and other personal regalia were returned to George III, and by the express command of William IV were deposited in the Crown Room in Edinburgh Castle in 1830 (see the photograph on page 28). (By permission of the Blairs Museums Trust.)

DID YOU KNOW. . .
that during the 1745 siege, the elderly governor of the castle, General Preston, went round the defences in his bath chair every two hours to keep the sentries on their toes? The only alarm, on the night of 25 September, proved false; the scrambling noise up the castle rock wasn't Jacobites - just goats grazing on the grassy tufts!

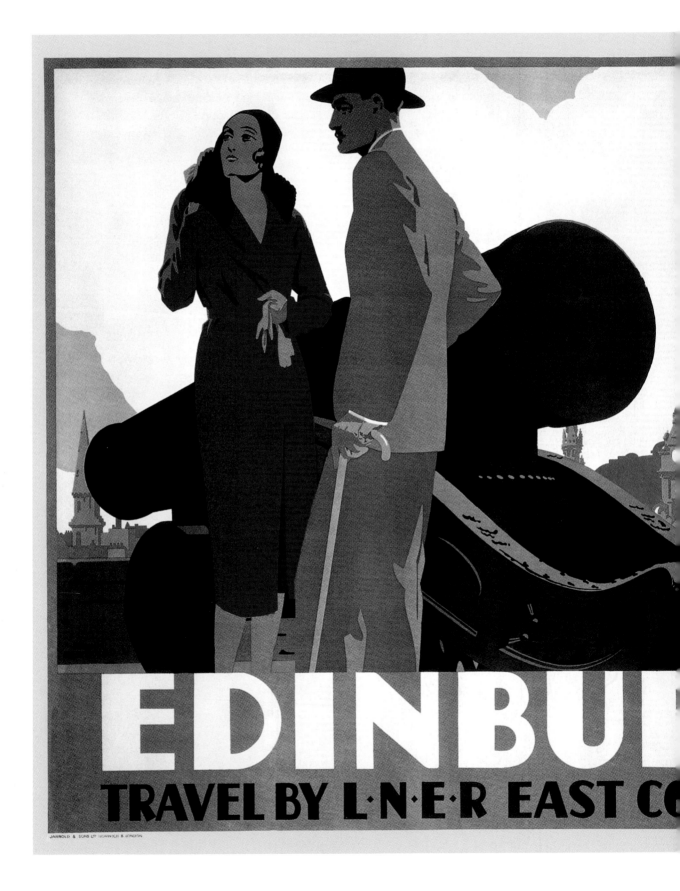

"Mons Meg"

ST ROUTE

Published by the LONDON & NORTH EASTERN RAILWAY

(By permission of the National Railway Museum/
Science & Society Picture Library.)

One morning in February 1818, Walter Scott watched with others as the Crown Room door was broken down and the locks of the great oak chest they found inside were burst open. There they discovered the ancient Honours of Scotland, exactly as they'd been left after the Treaty of Union with England 111 years earlier.

The Honours were immediately put on public display and among the first to visit them was George IV. His visit to Scotland in 1822 was the first by a reigning sovereign since Charles II in 1651.

The rediscovery of the Honours heralded a new use for the castle, as a visitor attraction, and Scott was soon immersed in another project - the return of Mons Meg from her 'exile' in the Tower of London. In March 1829, the great gun arrived at Leith, and from there was given a hero's welcome all the way to the castle battlements.

The momentum increased. In 1836 the Birthchamber in the Royal Palace was vacated by the army and opened to visitors. In 1846 St Margaret's Chapel was recognised among a clutter of buildings close to where Mons Meg had been placed. The later structures were swept away and the tiny chapel, the oldest building in the castle, was restored much as you see it today.

Other more grandiose schemes were projected for the castle. Most never got off the drawing board, including a proposal to build a memorial tower to Prince Albert, Queen Victoria's consort. But several projects were completed, including the new Gatehouse in 1888, and the restoration of the Great Hall in 1891.

The new role of the castle as ancient monument and visitor attraction was confirmed in 1905 when the War Office transferred responsibility for all the buildings to the Office of Works (now Historic Scotland).

DID YOU KNOW. . .
visitors in 1819 had to pay one shilling just to view
the Honours of Scotland? That's about £10 (16 Euros)
in today's money!

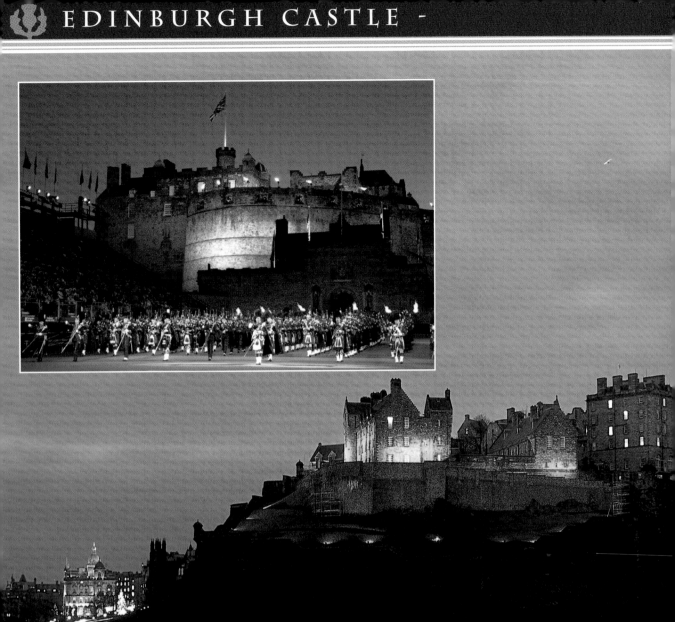

Today the ancient royal castle is as powerful a symbol of Scottish nationhood as it was in centuries gone by. It is an icon of Scotland's great medieval past, as well as the spiritual home of Scotland's proud military tradition.

The castle has also become the impressive backdrop and stage for some of Scotland's most important contemporary occasions - none more visually stunning than the world-famous Edinburgh Military Tattoo. What began in 1950 as a modest marching and countermarching of the pipes and drums back and forth across the Castle Esplanade has grown into one of the world's greatest spectacles, and the castle is never more alive than during the Edinburgh International Festival every August when the Tattoo is staged. Each tattoo closes with the appearance of the lone piper on the battlements of the castle - you'll be hard-pressed to find a dry eye in the house!

DID YOU KNOW. . .
Edinburgh Castle welcomes over 1,000,000 visitors every year? Not bad for a fortress chiefly designed to keep people out!

Left: Edinburgh Castle Rock from the west in late evening December 2002 - still going strong after 3000 years.
Inset: The Edinburgh Military Tattoo on the Castle Esplanade.

TIME - LINE

HOUSE OF MACMALCOLM

Malcolm III
(1058-93)

Donald III
(1093-7)
1093 St Margaret of Scotland, Malcolm III's widow, dies in Castle

Edgar
(1097-1107)
1107 King Edgar dies in Castle

Alexander I
(1107-24)

HOUSE OF BRUCE

HOUSE OF STEWART

Robert I
(1306-1329)
1314 Scots recapture Castle and Bruce orders its destruction

David II
(1329-1371)
1335 English recapture Castle
1341 Scots recapture Castle
1367 David II begins building David's Tower
1371 David II dies in Castle

Robert II
(1371-1390)
1384 First gun arrives in the Castle

Robert III
(1390-1406)
1398 Jousting tournament held at Castle
1400 Castle attacked by Henry IV of England

HOUSE OF STEWART *continued*

Charles II
(1649-1685)
1650 Honours of Scotland taken to Scone for Charles II's coronation on 1 January 1651
1650 Oliver Cromwell, Lord Protector of England, captures Castle
1660 Honours of Scotland returned to Castle
1681 Mons Meg breaks during salute for future James VII

James VII
(1685-89)

William & Mary
(1689-1702)
1689 Castle falls to supporters of William & Mary

Anne
(1702-14)
1707 Honours of Scotland locked away in Castle after Treaty of Union with England
1708 Queen Anne Building and Dury's Battery built after Jacobite Rising

HOUSE OF SAXE-COBURG & GOTHA/HOUSE OF WINDSOR

Edward VII
(1901-10)
1905 Castle transferred from War Office to Office of Works (now Historic Scotland)

George V
(1910-36)
1912 David's Tower rediscovered
1916-7 John Maclean and David Kirkwood, 'Red Clydesiders', imprisoned in Castle
1923 Army vacates Castle for Redford Barracks
1927 Scottish National War Memorial opened
1933 Naval and Military Museum (now National War Museum of Scotland) opened

Edward VIII
(1936)

George VI
(1936-52)
1939 First German POWs held in Castle after raid on Forth Bridge
1941-45 Honours of Scotland secretly buried in David's Tower
1950 First Edinburgh Military Tattoo held on Castle Esplanade